Eagles

Written by Deborah Hodge

Illustrated by Nancy Gray Ogle

KIDS CAN PRESS

WILDLIFE SERIES

Kids Can Press

For my mother-in-law, Ev Hodge, and her children and their families - DH
To my husband, Pat - NGO

I would like to gratefully acknowledge the review of my manuscript by Michael J. Chutter, Registered Professional Biologist and Bird Specialist with the British Columbia Ministry of Environment, Lands and Parks, Wildlife Branch.

I would also like to thank my editor, Lori Burwash, for her valuable help and kind suggestions. Thanks are also due to Valerie Hussey, my publisher; Valerie Wyatt, series editor; and Marie Bartholomew, series designer. In addition, I would like to recognize the efforts of the talented, hardworking staff at Kids Can Press. I am grateful to you all!

Text copyright © 2000 by Deborah Hodge
Illustrations copyright © 2000 by Nancy Gray Ogle

Kids Can Press acknowledges the financial support of the Ontario Arts Council, the Canada Council for the Arts and the Government of Canada, through the BPIDP, for our publishing activity.

Published in Canada by
Kids Can Press Ltd.
29 Birch Avenue
Toronto, ON M4V 1E2

Published in the U.S. by
Kids Can Press Ltd.
4500 Witmer Estates
Niagara Falls, NY 14305-1386

Edited by Lori Burwash
Designed by Marie Bartholomew
Printed and bound in Hong Kong by Book Art Inc., Toronto

CM 00 0 9 8 7 6 5 4 3 2 1
CM PA 00 0 9 8 7 6 5 4 3 2 1

Canadian Cataloguing in Publication Data
Hodge, Deborah
  Eagles

(Kids Can Press wildlife series)
Includes index.

ISBN 1-55074-715-0 (bound)   ISBN 1-55074-717-7 (pbk.)

1. Eagles — Juvenile literature. 2. Bald eagle — Juvenile literature. 3. Golden eagle — Juvenile literature. I. Ogle, Nancy Gray. II. Title. III. Series.

QL696.F32H62 2000   j598.9′42   C99-933009-8

Kids Can Press is a Nelvana company

Contents

Eagles

Eagles are big, powerful birds. They soar through the sky with their long, wide wings.

Eagles are birds of prey – birds who hunt for their food. All birds of prey have curved beaks and sharp claws.

A Bald Eagle's wings can spread up to 2.3 m (7 ½ feet) from tip to tip. This is longer than a bed.

Birds of prey
are also called
raptors.

Eagle claws are called talons.
The talons are used to kill
prey – the animals an eagle
eats. This Bald Eagle's foot is
the size of an adult's hand.

Eagles of the world

Eagles live on every continent except Antarctica. There are more than 50 species. Here are a few.

These **fish or sea eagles** live near water. They hunt for fish. Spikes on their feet help them hold their slippery prey.

African Fish Eagle

White-tailed Eagle

These **booted eagles** have leg feathers. Booted eagles often live inland. Some nest high in the mountains. They hunt rabbits, birds and other small animals.

Black Hawk-eagle

Martial Eagle

Short-toed Eagle

Bateleur

These **snake eagles** live in hot places, such as Africa. They eat snakes and other reptiles. Snake eagles have short toes for gripping their thin prey.

These **tropical eagles** are some of the biggest eagles. They live in rain forests. They hunt monkeys, sloths and large birds. Strong legs and feet help these eagles grab their heavy prey.

Harpy Eagle

Great Philippine Eagle

7

Eagles of North America

Two kinds of eagles live in North America – the Bald Eagle and the Golden Eagle. They are the largest birds of prey found here.

This is a young Bald Eagle. It will have adult coloring at age four or five years.

The Bald Eagle is a fish or sea eagle. The adult has white head and tail feathers. The Bald Eagle is about 76 cm (30 inches) tall – the height of a kitchen table. A large bird can weigh up to 7 kg (15 pounds).

The Golden Eagle is a booted eagle. The adult has golden feathers on its neck and head. It is about the size of a Bald Eagle. Like most birds of prey, female Golden Eagles are bigger than the males.

This is a young Golden Eagle. Its coloring is almost the same as the adult's above.

Where eagles live

Most eagles live in the wild. They need tall trees or cliffs for nesting and good areas for hunting. Many North American eagles live in the west.

Some eagles live in the same place all year. Others travel from one place to another as the seasons change. This is called migrating. Eagles migrate to find food.

Bald Eagles make their homes along rivers, lakes and seacoasts. Here, they can catch fish – their favorite food.

When rivers and lakes freeze over, Bald Eagles can't catch fish. They must migrate to places with open water.

Bald Eagles live only in North America. Golden Eagles also live in Europe, Asia and North Africa.

Golden Eagles can live almost anywhere in the wild. They are found in mountains, hilly areas or flat, open spaces.

Eagle food

Eagles hunt and kill other animals – their prey. They also feed on the remains of dead animals.

Golden Eagles' favorite food is rabbits and hares. They also hunt ground squirrels, marmots and grouse.

Bald Eagles eat fish. In the fall, they feed on spawning salmon – fish that lay their eggs and die. Bald Eagles also hunt water birds and other small animals.

If food is scarce, a Golden Eagle may attack a deer or other large animal.

Bald Eagles often steal fish from other birds, such as Ospreys.

An eagle kills its prey with its powerful feet. It tears off pieces of meat with its sharp beak and swallows them whole.

Eagle bodies

An eagle's body is made for flying and hunting. This is a Golden Eagle.

Eyes

An eagle sees two to three times better than a human. Its big eyes can spot prey up to 3 km (2 miles) away. A clear eyelid cleans and protects the eye.

Beak and jaws

The beak is as sharp as a knife. Powerful jaw muscles help the eagle crush and cut its prey. An eagle has no teeth. It swallows its food in chunks.

Legs and feet

Thick leg muscles help the eagle strike its prey. Long toes grip and crush. Sharp talons pierce the prey's body.

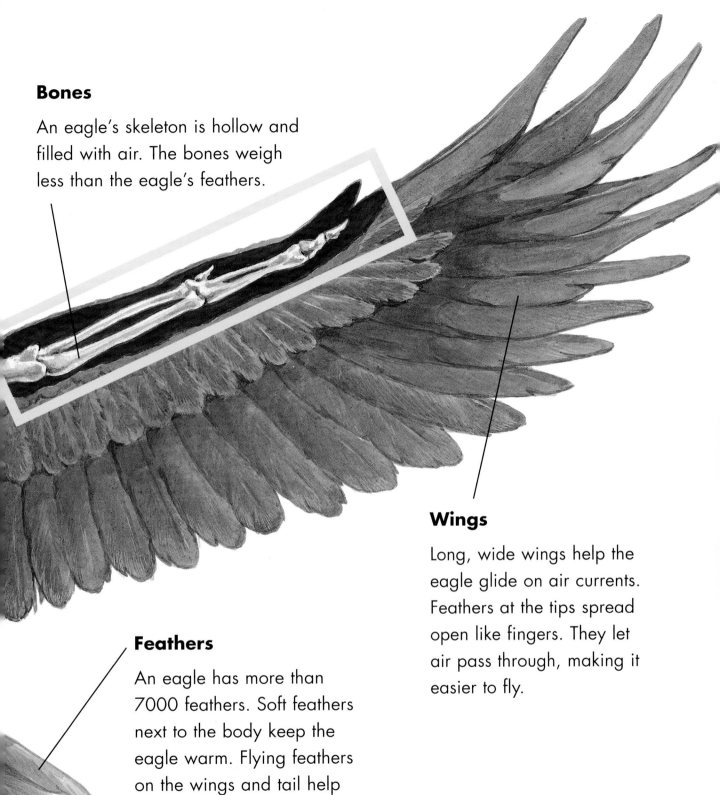

Bones

An eagle's skeleton is hollow and filled with air. The bones weigh less than the eagle's feathers.

Feathers

An eagle has more than 7000 feathers. Soft feathers next to the body keep the eagle warm. Flying feathers on the wings and tail help the eagle swoop and soar.

Wings

Long, wide wings help the eagle glide on air currents. Feathers at the tips spread open like fingers. They let air pass through, making it easier to fly.

How eagles fly

Eagles are strong, graceful fliers. They soar high in the sky.

Eagles can fly long and far without getting tired. They ride on thermals – warm air currents that rise from the ground. Eagles also glide on updrafts – winds that push up against mountains and hills.

Eagles fold their wings to dive for prey. When diving, a Golden Eagle can fly up to 190 km/h (120 miles per hour). This is about twice as fast as a car on a freeway.

EAGLE FACT

Migrating eagles fly about 55 km/h (35 miles per hour) – a little faster than a car on a city street.

Eagle nests

When an eagle is ready to lay eggs, she and her mate build a nest. Many eagles build their nests in the spring.

The nest is made with sticks. It is lined with soft leaves and grasses. Eagles often use the same nest each year. They add new sticks and grasses. Eagles make the biggest nests of any bird in North America.

Bald Eagles build their nest in a tall tree with sturdy branches. It is near water. Nests are often 2 m (6½ feet) across and 1 m (3 feet) tall – about the size of a small car.

Most Golden Eagles build their nests on rocky cliffs. Others nest in trees. A Golden Eagle's nest looks down on a good hunting area.

EAGLE FACT

One old Bald Eagle nest was 6 m (20 feet) high – as tall as a house!

Baby eagles

The mother eagle can lay up to three eggs, but she usually lays two. The eggs are laid a few days apart. The parents take turns sitting on the eggs. They keep them warm and safe. Bald Eagle eggs hatch in about 35 days.

To hatch, a baby eagle pecks at the shell from the inside. It uses a sharp "egg tooth" at the tip of its beak. A day or two later, the tiny eagle is out of the shell. The new baby is called an eaglet. It is weak and almost helpless.

Golden Eagle eggs take up to 45 days to hatch. The eggs are speckled. This helps them stay hidden from enemies.

The first eaglet is strong by the time the second egg hatches. If food is scarce, the older eaglet may kill the younger one.

This Bald Eagle warms the baby with her body. The second egg is beginning to hatch.

21

How eagles grow and learn

Eaglets are covered in soft down. Their parents keep them warm until longer feathers grow in. They feed the babies small pieces of meat. The oldest eaglet always eats first.

By age six weeks, eaglets can feed themselves. They hop around the nest and pounce on sticks. They stretch and flap their wings.

By ten weeks, eaglets are ready to fly, or fledge. The parents coax them from the nest with food. Soon, the young birds – now called fledglings – fly well. Their parents teach them to hunt. Two months later, young eagles may live on their own.

This eight-week-old Bald Eagle has new flying feathers. Soon it will be ready to fly!

Eaglets grow quickly. These Golden Eagle chicks are about three weeks old.

How eagles protect themselves

Adult eagles have no real enemies. Most animals are afraid of these big, strong birds. But eagle eggs and eaglets are in danger from many animals. Their enemies include raccoons, snakes, ravens, owls and other eagles.

Young eagles, living on their own, are at great risk. They battle hunger, harsh weather and older birds. Many eagles do not survive their first year.

When its parents go hunting, this young Golden Eagle must defend itself.

These Golden Eagle parents keep a close watch over the nest. If an enemy comes near, the parents scare it away.

Eagles and people

Over 100 years ago, people hunted eagles until few were left. Fifty years later, chemicals used on farmers' crops got into the eagles' food supply. Many eagles were sick. The shells of their eggs became soft. They cracked before hatching.

Today, there are laws to protect eagles. But as wild areas shrink, there are fewer places for eagles to live. Without a home, some die. Others move to cities if they can find food and trees for nesting.

A scientist puts a band on this young Golden Eagle's leg. Banding helps scientists count eagles and keep track of where they live.

Eagles can live in the wild for up to 30 years, but most die before they become adults.

Eagles need space to live and raise their young. People are working to save wild areas for eagles.

Other birds of prey

There are nearly 500 species of birds of prey in the world. Here are just a few.

Africa

Lappet-faced Vulture

African Pygmy Falcon

Secretary Bird

Australia

Letter-winged Kite

Europe and Asia

Eurasian Kestrel

North America

Red-shouldered Hawk

North America
Europe
Central America
Asia
Africa
South America
Australia

Central and South America

Crested Caracara

Worldwide

Osprey

Peregrine Falcon

Barn Owl

Eagle watching

Here are some things to look for if you go eagle watching.

Size
Eagles are bigger than other birds.

American Robin   Golden Eagle

Wings

A Golden Eagle from below   A Bald Eagle from below

Nests
A Bald Eagle nest
is usually found in
a tall tree.

A Golden Eagle nest is usually found
on a rocky cliff.

Talons
The talons shown on these pages are
the size of a real Bald Eagle's feet.
How do your hands compare?

Words to know

bird of prey: a bird with a hooked beak and talons that hunts other animals for its food

eaglet: a baby eagle

egg tooth: a sharp piece on an eaglet's beak used for pecking out of the shell. Once an eaglet has hatched, the egg tooth drops off.

fledge: to learn to fly

fledgling: an eaglet who has learned to fly but is still living with its parents

mate: a male or female partner in a pair of eagles. The pair produces babies each year.

migrate: to travel from one place to another as the seasons change

prey: an animal that is hunted for food

raptor: a bird of prey

talon: an eagle claw

Index